1 Am Life Itself

I am Life itself

Unmani * Liza Hyde

ISBN: 978-1-4303-1552-0

I don't know anything. I am completely lost. The one thing that I have always known is that I don't know. Throughout times when I thought I do know or I should know, or that everyone else seems to know, the one thing that has been the most dominant, the only constant, is that I don't know. Throughout the story of 'my life', there has always been the feeling of bewilderment, and not knowing. Then there has been the pretence of knowing, believing and hoping which appeared to cover this. This is all the play of Life.

Recognition of Life as it is, is recognition of what is already and has always been: not-knowing. This is what I am. Absolutely innocent not knowing. In not-knowing there is no doubt. In not-knowing there is absolute clarity. Simply the direct recognition of what is. This is what I am. I am Life itself.

Are You Sitting Comfortably...?

Once upon a time there was a little girl called 'me' (well, everybody else called her Liza). **This is simply a story** of what seemed to happen in time with a beginning, middle and an end.

When I was a child there was only this. Life happening. Nothing. Not-knowing. Innocence. I always knew this. Nothing ever happened. I saw the joke. I saw others pretending. Then fear arose and with it a sense of 'me in here' and 'them out there'. "What is expected of me?" "Must I play their game?" "I don't want to. I don't know how. What is this crazy world where everyone is pretending to be someones?" Confusion. Trying to fit in. Trying to survive. As I got to be a teenager confusion became confusion and rage. I was burning with rage against the pretence. Angry with the world. There was a feeling of something terribly, terribly wrong, something missing. All the time there was a subtle knowing of all that was happening, but at the same time this knowing was overlooked in the desperate trying to fit in.

I grew up in London in a semi-traditional Jewish South African family. I went to Jewish religious classes as a child where we learnt about how to follow the laws and how to pray to God. As a young child, I innocently enjoyed all of this and encouraged my family to be more religious. As I grew older I noticed the hypocrisy of religion. For example, on the Sabbath when God apparently says you must rest and not drive, my mother (and others) would drive to the synagogue and park around the corner, so that no one would see us and would think we had walked there! There were many lovely qualities about being part of a religion like spending a lot of time with all the family together and singing songs, but there also seemed to be many double standards. People talked about God, or being good, or having strong principles and morals, and at the same time this seemed to be just a show. In reality, I could feel confusion around me. Everyone seemed to be desperately hanging on to their belief in God and the Jewish traditions, as a last thread of hope that they would be saved. They felt safe in what was known. Generations have believed in God and followed these traditions, so who are we, to know any different?

I noticed this fear and rigidness almost everywhere. People seemed terrified to stand alone in Life. They seemed to rely on old beliefs and concepts because of the illusion of safety. As a child, I saw through all of this and felt very lost and confused.

I have a younger sister who is absolutely lovely. I always knew she recognised the nature of the innocence of Life. I never felt any separation from her. She is what I am. I just assumed that she recognised this as well and was so often amazed when she seemed to pretend to be a separate individual who seemed to need to prove and maintain her independence. She would push me away with a story based in fear and the idea of separation. As a teenager and young adult, I tried to reassure her in different ways, that I am what she is, but she often could not really hear or trust that. This meant that I often felt saddened and confused by this.

I felt so at home in the appearance of Life. When I was with my parents in a garden, my Mum or Dad would often say "Look, Liza, isn't that tree beautiful?" I would often answer with a kind of "Mmph" because I felt so angry. The trees, flowers and everything in the play of Life is my home. They are not special or beautiful. They are simply what they are—ordinary trees. Of course they are amazingly beautiful but this has nothing to do with a concept of beauty.

My parents used to say things like "Wasn't that great, yesterday?" and again I would feel cheated and confused. The past had never happened. I knew that it only exists as a memory. In fact all words seemed to be such a pretence. I didn't feel like talking much as I was growing up because I didn't know what to trust: the knowing that my nature is absolute innocence—which was sinking fast into the background, or the words that other people were saying. I innocently tried to play the game of words in order to survive in the world. I felt more and more confused and heartbroken. The feeling of an empty hole was felt as a physical sensation and an emotional story. I was waiting for a time when I would be able to trust what I know and maybe even find it reflected in the play of Life.

As a teenager, I exploded in rage at the world. My sweet parents felt the real brunt of this. I felt so heart-broken and empty. I felt that everything was meaningless and flat. I didn't care if I lived or died and would walk in front of cars in the middle of the road. My parents tried to help but they couldn't do anything right in my eyes. I could see through all the words and I felt they meant nothing. Although I acted very tough, actually I felt so lost.

I thought that I would be able to fill that empty hole or feeling of loss, with something in the play. I tried to find the ideal relationship, or career and I even thought that by analysing and working out the patterns of the thoughts with a psychologist, that I would 'work it all out'. I was searching for the missing link. That piece of the puzzle that would fill the emptiness and make the pain go away.

When I was 17 I left England and went to live in Israel on my own. This seemed like an attempt to rebel against authority and step into the unknown. In Israel, I went to University, enjoyed the beach, had a little black dog, felt very sad and angry very often, milked cows in a Kibbutz, had a few romantic affairs with soldiers, and some other experiences.

After seven years, I left Israel in a hurry to get away from the traumatically emotional end of a long relationship with an Israeli man, and flew to Japan. There I worked as a hostess in a nightclub and I entertained Japanese men by singing Karaoke with them and laughing at their jokes! After half a year there, I went off to Thailand for what I thought would be 3 months. But when I got there I met someone who said to me "Go to India now." I took this to mean something very significant and so promptly left Thailand for India. I arrived in India on my own, not knowing anything about India or where to go. Somehow I ended up living in India for most of 3 years. During this time I searched high and low on my so-called 'spiritual journey' as I lived and moved around India. The whole of India seemed to support my spiritual search. Everyone I met and everything that happened seemed to be so significant to me.

After several months of travelling around like this, I met a Nepalese/Indian man and fell hopelessly in love. At the time it felt like I was deciding between what seemed to be the mind and the heart. The mind seemed to be telling me that he was not the right kind of man for me (he was illiterate, ex-drug addict and generally seemed to be a dodgy character) but the heart was in love and asked no questions! The heart seemed to win and we ended up travelling and living together for over 2 years. We were such an unlikely couple, he was a Nepalese man pretending to be a 'cool' westerner and I was a

Western woman playing the role of an Indian wife. I wore saris and did puja (prayers and offerings) to the Hindu goddess Kali. As much as I enjoyed playing this role, after some time I had had enough. Around this time we happened to be travelling through Pune where the Osho Ashram is. My Nepalese boyfriend thought of Osho as like the devil and begged me not to go inside the Ashram. But once again I had fallen in love.

I loved hearing Osho speak (although it was only on video because he had been dead for 10 years). In lots of ways I remember thinking "This is my voice speaking" when I heard him speaking. Meditation was new for me and I loved it. I loved the inter-action with people in Pune and the 'juiciness' and almost open sexuality about the place. I loved the dancing and danced for hours every day. I received a new name from the women whom Osho had left in charge. I was given the name Unmani which in Sanskrit means 'no mind' or 'beyond the mind'. At the time I recognised that there is no significance to this name or any other name. I already knew that what I am is not a name. Having two names meant that I felt even less identified with the character 'me', that I had never really believed in. Even now, some friends call me Unmani and some, Liza. I don't have a preference because I am neither.

At the time, I still felt that I needed to improve something that was not quite right. I felt I needed to meditate and go deeper into myself even though at the same time I fought with feeling lazy and bored with meditation. I went up to the Himalayas and did a 10-day Vipassana silent retreat. There we sat in meditation for 10 hours every day. Although it seemed like a challenge, by the end of it I never wanted to speak again! However, I realised that the Vipassana technique was not for me when I heard that you need to continue to meditate diligently and persistently at least twice every day. I kept it up for about a month after leaving the retreat! It seemed to be such hard work which required much discipline. As lovely as it was, I knew that this was not *it*.

After that I went back to Pune and did a therapy group where we all regressed back to childhood to relive our pain for 5 days! This was basically a week of crying (not that my childhood was particularly traumatic at all). On the last day during a heavy catharsis session, I broke my ankle by attempting to kill my mother as I punched and kicked the mattresses and padded walls. This compounded my emotional state. As I sat in a wheelchair on the last day of the group, and listened to the therapist say "This has been just a taste of the work that you need to do on yourselves", **my world went black.** I felt so angry. It can't be this way. It can't be an endless digging into the past. It can't just be an endless search. **I know it's not.**

Because of my broken foot, I spent most of the

next month lying in bed staring up at the ceiling. I felt so lost and so at the end of my strength. The pain was physically and emotionally unbearable. It cannot be like this! I cannot go on like this. This cannot be all there is!

About a year before this, I had heard of a woman who was talking about 'Awakening'. When I first heard this term 'Awakening', I had no idea what it meant and I was not really interested in finding out. It seemed to be yet another spiritual experience or goal to be chased after. I already knew that these spiritual goals have nothing to do with actual fulfilment. But when I had heard more about what this woman was talking about, I felt terrified of going to see her because I realised that somehow this was the end.

As I lay in bed with my broken foot, I started to consider this. At the same time as being terrified, I knew that I couldn't go on like this. I was feeling pretty suicidal. Life was not worth living. All I wanted to do was numb the pain, sleep or die. So I went to see her.

As she spoke, I wrestled with what she was saying. I tried to work it all out. I tried to understand and relate what she said with what I thought I knew. Thoughts were looping and trying so hard to work out the answer.

At some point during this time, was a recognition of what I am. This is now seen to be what some people call 'Awakening'. I can't say that it was anything special because there was nothing and no one to describe it. After this non-event, thoughts tried to report back and explain that it happened because of this or that. But actually it simply happened. Or in fact nothing happened. It was actually the recognition of the absolute ordinariness of not-knowing, but with it there was a relaxation and so much relief in contrast to the desperation of seeking. It was seen that what was being pointed to is what I am. I have always known this but simply pretended that I don't know. I had become so used to over-looking it because it is always the background to all the pretence in this play of life. I had been so used to people pretending and talking about things that appear in the play and I had never realised that the play could be used to express that which knows the play. Once this was seen, there was only laughter. "Look, we are only pretending. Ha! Ha!" This is what people call an 'Awakening'. In fact you could almost say that there was a melting into what was **already known but only overlooked**. There were tears of gratitude—to Life. Finally, finally found. Finally reflected in the appearance. Finally the veil could fall away and there was only resting in not-knowing.

After this, a great relief was felt but there was sometimes doubt and still the questions of how to integrate this into my life, what do I do with this now? I spent some time up in the Himalayas and then went to Australia and New Zealand. I lived in Australia for about 2 years and had a fantastic time of practically no seeking. I lived in a tent for a while, I lived in a van for a while, I lived in a field for a while, and I lived on a beach for a while. At times this new perspective seemed to be slowly integrating itself, but then there were other times of confusion and doubt, when I felt drawn to other spiritual paths again. I went to New Zealand and again dabbled in various spiritual techniques because it seemed as if I could still improve something. Something still seemed to be slightly missing.

Soon after this I went back to London. One day, I went out for dinner with some friends and ended up having an argument with a male friend who accused me of being arrogant because I talked about 'Awakening'. I went home that night with my head spinning with thoughts. I doubted everything and almost agreed with him that I was being arrogant. Then as all the doubt built up into a mountain of doubt, it was recognised that all the doubt, confusion, arrogance, accusation, and everything, is what is, as well. There is no separation. There is not part of it that is, and part of it that isn't. There has never been a separate someone to be arrogant or not. I can say 'I am' or 'I know' and it is not arrogant, it is the way it is. I am the appearance of the separate character, as well as that which knows the character. There is no separation.

With this, there was a final relaxation. It was seen that actually, there is only arrogance at the same time as absolute humility. But the belief in a someone who owns this had fallen away. With this, fell away all confusion and trying to become. There was no actual event to mark a specific moment, but a melting away of belief and assumptions. When described in words, it can sound like something special happened but this is the way of words and thoughts. They dramatise. Actually nothing ever happened. I am all that is, and has ever been.

This is what some people call 'Enlightenment' or 'Liberation'. But I cannot say that "I am Liberated" because it has nothing to do with 'me'. In fact, there is no longer any idea of a separate 'me' who could do anything, especially not achieve any state of 'Liberation'. 'Liberation' is simply a word which points to the recognition of absolutely nothing. There is nothing to achieve and no one to achieve it. I don't know anything. But out of not knowing, is complete knowing. I am completely lost, and out of that there is a delight in whatever happens. I am forever falling and never land. This is absolute freedom. There is only 'Liberation'. I wouldn't choose such a fancy word, though. It is much too simple for that. It is simply Life. **I am simply Life**.

I am Life itself

Life is. There is no one living it. It is not 'my life'. There is no 'me' that lives. But I am Life. This 'I' is not a personalised 'me'. It is not an assumed separate person. There is no implied separation between the writer and the reader. This 'I' is 'you'. This 'I' is all that is. I am Life itself.

That I am Life itself, is known. This knowing goes beyond knowledge and intellect. This knowing is a knowing beyond experience, beyond thought or emotion. *Knowing in not knowing.* I don't know how I know, except that, I am. There is no doubt. As this knowing of what I am, the character goes on playing the game of being a character in a play. The play is no longer taken seriously, but still everything can and does happen. It is simply known that whatever happens does not happen 'to me'. It simply happens in, and as, what I am.

These words are not pointing to anything new. In fact what is being expressed here is timeless. It has always been known. It is known. It is most familiar and ordinary. It is what I am.

The following pages have been inspired by dialogues with a few lovely people about the various misconceptions and confusions to do with the nature of Life and 'Liberation'.

Who the Hell Am I?

Have you ever had to fill in one of those annoying questionnaires that ask you to describe yourself and your personality? I sit there wondering who they want me to describe! Which personality do they mean? Who the hell am I anyway? What comes to mind is the personality that my parents or others have told me I am. The personality that I have assumed myself to be. This involves a life history, which I could regurgitate from memory in the same way as always. "I was born in..., I grew up...I did this...I did that..." Or I could list some qualities that people have said I am. "I'm a shy person, I'm enthusiastic, I'm friendly, I'm sensitive..."

But am I just a list of qualities or past memory? No, but without that, what else am I? Most people are terrified to look at what they are (or in fact what they aren't!). When it is really recognised that there has only been an assumption of a 'someone', all that is left is emptiness. There is nothing left to hold on to. This can seem terrifying because it is Death. Death of the 'someone'. In recognition there is no fear. When it is recognised that there never has been a 'someone', there is also a realisation that the whole story is just a joke!

The Spiritual Path

There is a multitude of ways of pretending to try to avoid not knowing what I am. One way is the spiritual path. It is such a beautiful and exciting way.

The path, by its very nature is about becoming. "This is not it; there must be something more. There must be something more significant and meaningful than this. This path will lead me somewhere one day (hopefully never!)." The path is driven by a longing for fulfilment. Fulfilment is always over there in the future, if I do this or that. I never actually want to find what I'm looking for because that will be the end of the spiritual path. There is such a love and addiction to the seeking.

The spiritual path is about other people's authority. "They must know and I couldn't possibly know". "I must follow what they say, so I can become as enlightened as they are". Spiritual teachers tend to perpetuate this master-disciple relationship by trying to teach and help us poor, lowly, unenlightened creatures. By suggesting that I need to do something or become something, they are reinforcing the idea that I am separate.

There are spiritual teachers who teach meditation or say to stop judging. There are teachers who say that the way to fulfilment is to express your emotions. There are teachers who say that if you stop thinking then you will become enlightened. Some say that the Universe will provide and that Mother Earth loves you. Others say that if you return to your true self as man or woman and make love properly then you may have the final orgasm. Most teachers imply or say directly that there are steps towards a hazy final goal that can be attained only by the honoured special ones and for the rest of us it is something to strive for eternally. Possibly by the end of the next life we might be a bit closer to it!

This is all such a beautiful story but nothing to do with the way it actually is. Seeking is simply a game that is played until the recognition that there is nothing to find.

It seems extraordinarily arrogant to actually say that I am already all that I seek to become. Nearly everyone is searching for something or trying to improve themselves in some way, that it seems unbelievable that I could say that I'm absolutely perfect just like this. What I am is absolutely fulfilled and has never been touched by any notion that I'm not.

The carpet has already been ripped out from under my feet. In fact the whole floor has gone and I am falling. There is no one. No one can decide to meditate or stop thinking. No one can decide to express their emotions or stop judging. Even if I did do any of these things they would have nothing to do with recognising what I am. I could just as well be playing mini-golf or smoking a cigarette.

The Seeker

How beautiful is the play, which plays not knowing what it truly is. Out of this beautiful play of pretence arises an individual who plays trying to find herself. The seeker tries to find her true nature, thinking that it is possible to find the answer in the play itself. The seeker tries to find the unfindable within the find-able. It is impossible to find because it is that which pretends to seek itself. It is not anything specific; it is specifically everything, including the seeker herself. It is like trying to see my own eyes. I can't see them because they are what is seeing. Seeking is Life play-ing at seeking itself.

While it appears that 'I am seeking', there seems to be a path towards an imagined idea of fulfilment. Things happen in the play, which seem to signify very important and special steps towards a final goal. There seems to be a growing or flowering. This is all absolutely, beautifully, perfectly wonder-ful as well as beautifully, perfectly disappointing. At each apparent step of this spiritual path, there is such hope, which is followed by great disappointment. Hope, that *this* is the step that is the *true* way to fulfilment, and disappointment at the discovery that actually, this is not it. But not to worry, the next hopeful step shows its head pretty soon and the path goes on. The seeker actually loves to seek. She is not interested in being found.

Seeking is such a beautiful game. There seems to be such desperation to know. It can seem so painful. The thoughts seem to fight with letting go. Ideas that there is something to do or find, contradict the knowing that there is nothing to do and nowhere to go. There is such fear but also such attraction to falling into not knowing. It often feels like all that is known and familiar is crumbling and that can feel terrifying. It is such an exciting drama of thoughts and emotions. Although it can be incredibly painful, it is also an addictive drug that cannot be given up. The seeker cannot give up itself. Seeking is actually just another way of keeping up the pretence that I am hiding from what I am. The struggle goes on, until it stops.

Then it is recognised that there is no individual seeker. The whole pretence is seen for what it is. There never was a seeker. There was never any path to go anywhere. **There is nowhere to go**. There is nothing to seek. What is being sought *is* even in the seeking itself.

The Fucked Duck

One day I was walking on the Heath with a couple of friends and we saw a duck that had its foot caught in a branch in the water. It was struggling in great panic to free itself. It would struggle for a few moments and then rest for a while and then again struggle to free itself. As we watched this duck struggling, all three of us realised that there was really nothing we could do to help this duck. It was stuck right in the middle of a large lake. None of us were going to jump into the cold, murky water and swim out to rescue the duck. None of the other ducks that were swimming around even seemed to notice the fucked duck's plight. As we watched we considered that the only way we might be able to help would be to throw a large rock at it to put it out of its misery. But then, who knows, it might be able to free itself eventually on its own—perhaps if it simply relaxed. We stood there for quite some time, watching with wonder at the duck's struggle for freedom.

I realised that the struggle of this fucked duck was a beautiful analogy for the desperate seeker. Caught in a trap, the seeker struggles for freedom. The onlooker, who knows the plight of the seeker, knows also that there is no way to help him. All the onlooker can do is watch in wonder at the struggle, recognising that **the struggle is only absolute Freedom pretending to struggle**. This play of struggle will certainly lead to the end of the struggle, either as freedom in Life, or Death. Either way, it does not matter. There is already only Freedom.

Nothing to Teach

There is no one to teach, no one teaching and nothing to teach. This is already known. It already is all that is. It is already absolutely perfect. There are no seekers; there are no 'Liberated' ones. There are only appearances. There is nothing for the seeker to search for, but searching is the play of Life. Even though the seeker goes on seeking, the innocence that is Life waits patiently to be recognised. There is no need for recognition of the nature of Life or 'Liberation'. Life is already all that it could ever be. It simply plays the role of the individual seeker for a while.

Then there are apparently those who 'wake up'. To the seeker, it appears that the individual has become special and experiences life in a more desirable way. The seeker believes that the 'Liberated' one can teach them how to become fulfilled. In recognition of what I am, it is seen that there is no individual, there is absolute fulfilment already, but this is not seen in the way that the seeker has been looking. It is a leap from something, into nothing and everything. There is only Life squirming around, appearing as a multitude of appearances. It is already whole. Nothing is lacking. Even the pain and desperation of the seeker is exactly perfect. Everything is absolutely ordinary. It is only thought and imagination that creates something special. In reality, there is only the simplicity of Life being Life.

Listening to talk of 'Enlightenment'

Throughout history there have been accounts of certain people with special powers or those who have reached a special state of consciousness, who seem to stand separately and above the rest of the regular people. These 'special people' have often tried to help the regular ones by trying to explain how they achieved this state or even by trying to give some special offering of energy from this state. The regular people then try to do whatever has been recommended in order to reach this state (which has also been recommended).

This is so full of misconceptions, but is what so many spiritual seekers believe. Apparently 'Enlightened people' seem to describe what 'Enlightenment' or 'Liberation' is like. They use words like 'the end of all suffering', 'ease', 'unconditional love', 'freedom from bondage', 'causeless joy' and the innocent seeker tries to create or copy these ideas in order to become 'Enlightened' or 'Liberated'. The seeker assumes that these are qualities that the 'Enlightened person' owns. Actually what is being described is what *is already* and is common to all appearances but never owned by any appearance. The seeker assumes that the 'Enlightened' or 'Liberated' person's experiences are special in some way. What is heard and what is actually said is most often worlds apart. The seeker always hears through the earmuffs of seeking.

Life is never owned by anyone, no matter how 'Enlightened' they are. 'Enlightenment' is recognised beyond the appearance of the body/mind. The body/mind is simply an appearance in this. In this recognition, the body/mind is not more special. There is a tendency for there to be a more natural way for the body/mind, a general ease and relaxation. But this does not mean that discomfort, irritation, anger, pain cannot happen.

In the simple recognition of Life as it is, there are no more words that can describe the way it is. But this does not mean that it is so special. Actually it is the opposite, it is more ordinary than before. All the specialness has fallen away and what is left is what has always been—absolutely nothing.

An 'Enlightened person'

We often want to place experience and people in a definable box so that we can label the box and then everything that is spoken or done by this person is interpreted through the box. This feels safe and makes sure that everything is known. If someone is talking about 'Enlightenment' or 'Liberation' or 'Awakening', we want to know whether they are truly 'liberated' before we can start to hear what it is they are saying. If they say 'I am liberated' or even if it is believed that they are liberated, then from then on what is heard, is heard through the listener's interpretation of what that means. It is an image of what a 'liberated' person must be like. It often includes kindness, generosity, meditative, compassion, purity and other such special qualities.

Most spiritual teachers fit nicely into the box of what is imagined. They might wear white, they might sit very still, they might talk really slowly, they might close their eyes a lot.

If an apparently 'Enlightened person' does something which does not fit in the boxed idea of a 'Enlightened person', such as getting angry, or smoking a cigarette, then either the seeker goes to another spiritual teacher who fits better with their idea of a 'Enlightened person' or the box explodes.

In what I am there is no box. There is no safety.

Everything is exposed. There is no definable box of a character. Anything can happen. Sitting with eyes closed can happen or bursting into tears can happen. Nothing is more significant than anything else. There is simply what happens. There are no rules. There are no limits.

To say that 'I am an Enlightened person' is absolutely ridiculous. It is just as ridiculous as saying 'I am a dusty old file which is neatly filed in a cabinet'. This filing of a concept in a box and labelling it means that it can be found again when I need to compare other concepts to it. Without labels or boxes, what reference points would I have? What else would there be? **It could be very dangerous...**

Nothing

Nothing as a word or concept seems like a dead, dry emptiness. What is being pointed to here is not a concept of nothing. It is not anything. Not an imagination of nothing. Absolutely nothing. This can seem terrifying. We hold on so tightly to being something, because we know that really there is only nothing. This nothing has no boundaries or limits. It is boundless. It is endless. It is beyond concepts of time or space.

Closed eyes and there is only nothing. There is only sensation felt in nothing. This nothing is the emptiness in which everything happens. This nothing is alive. Open eyes and there is a rush of visual perception. Nothing overflows as everything. Eyes closed or open, **the fabric of Life is alive nothingness.**

The Dream

Throughout my life I had often felt that this is all just a dream. Sometimes things just didn't really seem real or as significant or meaningful as they pretended to be. But people around me whom I loved and respected seemed to take everything so seriously. Finally, in recognition of Life itself, it is seen that this sense that I always had, was true. This is all a dream. All experience, all thought, all emotion, all sensation, all appearance is simply a dream. It is the same as a dream that happens in sleep at night except that this dream is assumed to be real. This is just a 'surround–sound', '3D' dream. In sleep there is absolutely nothing, and then dreaming happens in that. When waking up in the morning happens, actually this is a 3D dream happening in absolutely nothing as well. No one wakes up.

The dream happens and in the dream is a character called 'me'. The character 'me' plays along with other dreamt characters like actors on a stage. Life dreams the dream and plays all the characters including the stage, the set, the lighting and the audience.

Life experiences itself in a multitude of forms and experiences. Life appears as an individual character that experiences individual experiences. Actually there is no separate individual *in* the character. The character has just assumed itself to be a separate individual which lives in a body. One could say 'how arrogant of this individual to presume to own Life', but it is all absolutely perfect. This assumption is Life experiencing itself assuming to be an individual. This is the play of separation. It makes no difference to Life, whether the thought 'I am a separate individual' is assumed or not. Life goes on dreaming itself. In fact it makes no difference to Life, whatever happens in the dream. It is always a dream. The character plays any role, anything can happen and it is always Life itself.

In recognition of the nature of Life, the dream is seen as a dream. It is no longer taken to mean anything. There is no longer a belief in any character called 'me'. Nothing happens 'to me' anymore. It is seen that the 'me' is the dream as well. This is a completely new and radical perspective in that which has always been known.

The Wish for Things to be Different

Seeking is all based on the wish for more than simply what is. Dreaming. Vaguely believing that everything will get better one day. What is, is unsatisfactory, unacceptable and, quite frankly, not perfect enough. Thoughts and dreams about more perfect future situations seem much more attractive than nothing but what is. 'If only what is was a little bit more shiny, or didn't have that bit of dirt in it, it would be perfect!'

This wishing for things to be different than what is, is the game of seeking and disappointment in never finding. It is the veil which seems to cause what is to be overlooked. **Nothing will ever be better than this**. This is all there is. There is nothing else. There is no hope. There is no more.

Thoughts and imagination will always want more than what is. This is their nature. But what I am, knows all thought. What I am sees all seeming imperfection and wish for perfection. What I am does not care whether there is a wish for things to be different or not—it is always simply what is.

Unique Perception

Each unique perception or character has to rediscover the nature of Life for itself. Life lives as unique perceptions within the play. Each one is absolutely alone. From each perception there are no others. There is only Life happening from this perception. No matter what appears, the unique perception is absolutely alone and can never be reached within the play. No one can ever reach that aloneness and sense of loss that each unique perception feels. This is the empty hole that can never be filled. This is the longing to find the perfect lover who will be able to reach that aloneness. The unique, alone seeker longs to find that, which can complete him or her. It can be terribly painful.

This is the appearance of separation. It appears that I am separate from the rest of the world out there. It is also assumed that there are other people with other perceptions, even though this can never be known. While there is this belief, there is a longing or a seeking for what is always beyond any belief.

All there is, is *this* perception. Perception is not owned by a someone or by a body/mind. Perception just is. All that is perceived, is just appearing in perception. All appearances are simply perception, including the appearance of this body/mind or that chair. There is no separation.

I am absolutely alone. There are no others. There is not even a character 'me'. The character 'me' is also part of perception. Thoughts are perceived. Emotions are perceived. It is all perceived. What perceives is Life itself. Life perceives the whole play. I am Life and as this, I am the play of whatever happens. The play is a play of boundaries. The play has limits. There appears to be a body and it can't walk through walls. The play is governed by rules of science. Cut me and I bleed. The play is a play of duality. There appear to be many people and many things happening to them. There appears to be cause and effect. It is a brilliant play of genius. It is the play of nothing appearing as everything.

Within perception, there is a body/mind that feels a sense of loss. It tries to find something within perception which can fill the loss. This goes on until it is finally recognised that, that loss can never be filled by something in perception. That which perceives the play has no boundaries. That which knows all that appears knows that it all is just happening in free-falling Life. That which perceives never lacks and has never been touched by any feeling of loss.

The unique perception and that which perceives are one. When there is seeking and a belief in a separate 'me', there are blinkers and only a contracted personal view is perceived. Only this unique perception knows home for this apparent seeker. No one else can describe it. No one else can know it. It is the most intimate and familiar recognition. That is why sometimes it seems that in recognition, the unique perception finally knows the **courage to stand alone and roar!**

True Authority

I am the one. I am the only authority. **I know.** I am. This knowing is all that is. Knowing is all that is worth trusting. There is nothing else. I am all that is and therefore the only authority on everything and nothing.

But who am *I* to know? Surely only the great sages or wise men can truly know but not little ol' me? Surely only those who have meditated for years or lifetimes can attain true knowing? Surely only those who have worked on themselves in therapy or healing could become whole? What about aligning the chakras or opening my heart? Surely it takes years or lifetimes to do that? What about those who sit in the most enlightened yoga position for ages? Surely I'm not ready right now, I need to work hard at something in order to get somewhere! Surely what everyone else seems to be looking for can't be what I already am!

Everything is absolutely perfect just the way it is right now. I am already absolute fulfilment. That includes all imperfect thoughts, all laziness about meditation, all issues that haven't been dealt with in therapy, all unaligned chakras and unopened hearts! I am already all that is. There needs no improvement. What I am has no chakras, nor heart, nor issues. What I am is boundless. I am absolute perfection that knows the play of imperfection and perfection.

It Can't Be That Easy

After searching for fulfilment or enlightenment for years, to be told that I am already fulfilled and enlightened seems to be too easy. 'Surely it must be something more, something very spiritual.' Enlightened people should act a certain way and look a certain way. They should be vegetarian and not smoke or drink. Enlightened people are people who have attained a special spiritual state after years or lifetimes of meditation and self-enquiry. They have dissolved all their karmic knots and opened all their chakras. This shows in their compassion and their aura of unconditional love for mankind.

This is a lovely image. I'm sure someone can act the 'Enlightened master' really well and end up having lots of disciples. They might enjoy holding on to this image but it does seem like hard work.

Why would Life be anything but easy? There is just the assumption that it has to be difficult because in the play, when I want to achieve something, it seems that I need to work hard at it. The nature of Life is not difficult. Look at a flower; does it work really hard to be a flower? Does it need to hold the image of 'flower' in order to be a flower? What is being pointed to here is simply Life recognising itself. Life being Life. Flower being flower.

It's so easy that it's already all just happening by itself!

Absolute Innocence

I am pure innocence. I am child-likeness. I am pure love. I am empty. I am absolute wholeness. I am sweetness in everything that appears and that does not. I don't know anything but there is knowing of everything. Love is the innocent essence of all that is. Everything that appears is screaming its existence in sweet simplicity. The chair is unabashedly screaming, "I am chair!" Sheep in a field stop and look at me as I pass and in their eyes they say, "I am sheep". Simple as that. It is all just the way it is. The clouds in the sky are unashamed to be naked. They scream, "I am cloud!" They are like a woman who stands unashamed and naked in the middle of a football field screaming "I am what I am!"

Thoughts seem to hide and control. Words protect and defend. What is there to hide from? Not knowing? Never finding the answer? But what a longing to stand naked in the middle of the football field of Life. It's already happening. This is the **roar of Life!** This roar jumps beyond hiding and protecting. This is absolute powerful innocence. It is all screaming. Everything screams aliveness. Everything screams that this is it—Life and Death all in one.

Protection

We go around pretending to protect the sweet intimate innocence that we are, assuming that it is private and personal. We feel terribly lost and alone. There seems to be an outside that wants to hurt that innocence which is assumed to be inside. There are all means of hiding and protecting - logic and talk, lashing out in emotions, all kinds of stories are played out. All this to try to protect that which seems to be too fragile and sweet for the 'big bad world'. At the same time there is a longing for a resting place. A place where we can stop trying to protect and can just relax.

There is the assumption that this resting place can be found in the play. So we look for it in other people; we look for it in career fulfilment; we look for it in spiritual practices and experiences. There is so much energy put into this protecting that if it wasn't for sleep at night we would become exhausted.

In any case at some point there is absolute exhaustion and desperation. Any resting place in the play is recognised to be only temporary. Nothing is satisfactory anymore. Nothing means anything. There is no way left to protect. Everything crumbles and falls apart. The sweet innocence, which was thought to be private and personal, is exposed. It is recognised that it is not personal at all. This was simply an assumption. It was simply a case of mistaken identity.

This sweet innocence is all that is. There is no end to it. There is no need to protect 'myself' within this, because I am all that is. All assumed boundaries fall away and all that is left is final resting as the absolute innocence of what I am.

The Owner

The belief that there is a 'someone' who can 'own' something happens in most apparent individuals. Everything that happens in the play is put on a scale of 'how does this affect me?' The idea of an owner means that whatever happens is owned or 'happens to me'. Actually, whatever happens, simply happens. The owner is only an idea that has been believed without question.

Where is this phantom owner? *Who* is this owner? There is no owner and nothing has ever been owned. Who owns this thought? Who owns this piece of cheese? Who owns this image of body? Who owns this emotion? Everything just happens without belonging to anyone. Without meaning or significance. Absolute impersonality.

I'm So Special

Feeling 'I'm special' can happen both in a positive (I'm so great) way and in a negative (I'm not good enough) way. People often think that they have a particular problem that makes them special. 'My special problem is that I'm too insecure, and that is why it is particularly difficult for me.' 'My special problem is that I had such a hard childhood.' 'My special problem is that I was abused.' 'My special problem is that people just don't understand me.'

There is enjoyment of the story of a special definition. It gives meaning and reasons for things that happen. Without it what else is there? Nothing, no definition, and that feels terrifying. From that special story comes the feeling of loneliness, of separateness. 'No one can ever understand 'me'. What a 'poor me' story! This is simply an addiction. It is an addiction to the story of 'me' because without 'me', I am lost.

However, what is so often overlooked is that, **Life is already lost**. It is too late to try to be in control. Even if I seem to be addicted to the story of 'me', beyond that, it is always known that this is just a play. In the seemingly hardest moments, what I am is never touched by any hardship. I am not limited to any particular special story. I have no boundaries or definition. This is already known but is absolutely not special. If this *is* special, then everything is special.

Everything *is* special. The way the raindrops sparkle on leaves, the way these fingers go 'tap, tap, tap' on the keyboard, the feeling of sadness, the feeling of irritation, looking into beautiful eyes, ... There is no end to how special everything is in the simplicity of what is. Thoughts tend to blow things out of proportion and add extra shiny bits to everything. But even without any extra anything, this is absolutely, perfectly special.

Words

Words seem to make simple things complicated and elaborate. They make basic things seem special and 'wow!' I grew up to believe words and believed that things are as words imply. I believed that that way I could escape the fact that Life is a lot more ordinary than words make out. It is ordinary, but absolutely beautiful in a way that words can never touch. Words just seem to skim across the surface of Life. Belief in words (and thoughts) never seems to be enough, though. It is always known that there is more to Life than just words. This is known beyond words and thoughts. Words are used to reach out for more, but they never seem to be able to grasp anything. **Life beyond words can never be grasped**. Words split one into two - before and after, you and me, in and out, here and there. This is all that words can do. They are the language of duality.

When listening to words, they are often taken to mean something completely different to their meaning. What is heard is simply what the individual can hear and no more and no less. What one individual hears is absolutely unique and perfect for them and has no bearing on what another individual hears, or even on what is said, for that matter. It is the same with reading words on paper. Each unique individual takes in only what they can take in. Words are simply happening as part of the play and actually have no meaning. They are different sounds vibrating with meanings seemingly attached to them. We use words to communicate with others within the play. Ultimately, there is no need to communicate since there are no others, there is only Life.

But the play of words goes on, and sometimes words can point directly to what is impossible to describe in words. When the individual can hear them pointing, then the body/mind can be touched with the joy of recognition. This is Life recognising itself.

Intellectual Games

Often when I am around people having an intellectual conversation I tend to zone out and don't really pay attention to the words but I love listening to the sound of their voices and watching the expressions on their faces. It is fascinating to watch how serious they take it. It is all a game of trying to use the 'right' words and pretending that 'I know'. It is especially fascinating and amusing to watch people talk about concepts of 'Awakening' or 'Non-duality' seriously and intellectually.

'Awakening' and 'Non-duality', by their very definition, are words which point to the oneness of Life itself beyond any dissection by words. However, these words and concepts are often played around with in intellectual games. This can seem very confusing (as well as quite boring and annoying!) for the seeker, who can assume that they need to understand these intellectual games in order to understand or be worthy of 'Awakening'. Recognition of Life has nothing to do with intellect. Recognition has nothing to do with trying to use the 'right' words and sound clever. This is only another way of seeming to avoid Life itself in not knowing.

Cleverness and intellectuality can be great fun and often are games that are played to avoid recognising that **I know nothing and am totally lost and bewildered**. Pretending to know a lot and therefore trying to control Life with words and ideas is the pretence that 'I can be safe'. Trying to 'fit in' and 'get it right' and use the 'right' words are all part of this intellectual game based in the fear of revealing the fact that really, **I just don't know**.

In Life there is never anything I can do wrong. There is never a need to try to get anything right. Words will always be wrong. Words can never touch the sweetness of Life itself. Words simply point. So what if I say the 'wrong' words or do the 'wrong' thing. What I am does not care about any concept of right or wrong. Recognition of what I am jumps beyond any right or wrong words or concepts.

There can never be the right words for Life happening, anyway. Non-duality or Advaita or Awakening or Liberation are long, clever-sounding words which point to absolute innocent not knowing. This is Life. This needs no word to describe it since every word and no words are it already.

Everything and Nothing

Everything is nothing and nothing is everything. This is the paradox which can never be understood. Nothing is happening as everything. Everything that happens, happens in nothing and as nothing. There is no separation between everything and nothing. There is only one. Chair is nothing happening as chair. Thought is nothing happening as thought. Idea of 'me' is nothing happening as idea of 'me'. Even the imagination of nothing is nothing happening as imagination of nothing!

There is only absolute emptiness. Emptiness is also absolute overflowing fullness. There are no boundaries in emptiness. There are no boundaries or limits in absolutely nothing. There are also no boundaries or limits to the fullness of everything as nothing. Knowing this is a freedom beyond any apparent restriction. Knowing this is the ordinary and natural freedom of what I am.

This Has Always Been Known

This has always been known. Even when there is a belief in a separate individual, this is known. Even though the perception is a contracted and narrow one (like a horse with blinkers), that which knows all perception, knows a contracted perception. It is known but it is not recognised as that which is the substance of everything. It is in the background seemingly hidden beneath a bundle of beliefs and assumptions. It is always longed for but also feared because the exciting story of the individual will be revealed as just a farce.

I have always had a feeling that this is all fake. That I play a role but actually what I am is that which knows the playing. What I am is never touched and has never been touched, no matter what has happened. No matter what pain or suffering I appear to have experienced, **what I am has never been touched**. No matter what is believed or assumed, this, that I am, does not even care. Even if I believe that I am totally unenlightened, what I am is still absolute enlightenment.

This has always been known as the most familiar, intimate knowing. So familiar that it is overlooked. So simple that it is dismissed in the search for something special. It is never usually directly pointed to in the play of life. Actually, it cannot truly be described or pointed to because it is beyond all words and concepts. It does not have the limits that all words imply. It is so sweet and untouched that it can feel as if talking about it might spoil it. But there is such a longing to find it in the play, that when it is recognised and no longer overlooked, it is like coming home to what has always been known.

Recognition

This cannot be understood. It can only be recognised. Until recognition, there can be a trying to understand or grasping at the words, which are pointing to what is beyond words. Recognition cannot be forced and no particular circumstances are necessary. But there can be a tiring of trying to understand that which can never be understood. Sometimes it can take years before trying to understand is exhausted. Sometimes this only needs to be heard once or sometimes there is recognition 'out of the blue' with no apparent connection to anything in the story.

In recognition there is never any connection to anything that has come before this. In recognition, there is no story of past or future. There is no time. Any apparent story is recognised as simply a story. Nothing causes recognition because any apparent cause is simply a story. Recognition is the end of the belief in the story. Recognition is a leap beyond concepts. Beyond belief. Beyond what has always been assumed. It is a leap into the unknown. It is a leap into what has always been known but simply overlooked. I can recognise what is being pointed to in these words, because I am that. This is what I am, beyond any story of 'me'. This is how I know that which is pointing, and that that is pointing to what I am.

Aliveness

Life is happening right now in this. Bum on chair. Fingers click-clacking on keyboard. Sound of wind blowing. Just sound or sensation happening. It is all so alive. **Life is throbbing with raw, sexual, aliveness.** Everything is squirming. Every sense is alive with sensation. There is nothing more or better than this. Nowhere to go. No escape. This is Life. This is Aliveness.

Scientifically, Life is about reproduction. But this is happening beyond the concept of it. Making love happens in every moment. The play of Life is actually Life making love with itself in all that happens. This is Aliveness. I can't do it, or make it happen. It is happening already. It is absolutely beyond my control. It is completely out of control!

Aliveness is a raw sexuality, which can seem terrifying. It exposes all pretence of individuality. There is the fear that it will overwhelm 'me' and I try to suppress it, but it can't be suppressed. It bursts out everywhere all the time. Even 'suppressing' is Life making love to the idea of suppressing!

It is very dangerous. So dangerous, that it is the death of 'me'. The pretence of an individual burns up in this fire of Life-love-making!

Thoughts and Mind

Thoughts arise and fall away. What is the problem? They are just doing their job. The function of thought is to think. It does a fantastic job at that! Imagination, which is also thoughts appearing as images, is brilliant. Reasoning, imagination, thought stories, all help the individual play in the play. Some teachers imply that thinking is wrong and that a 'quiet mind' or no thought is best. I was so ready to agree with them in the past because I felt how painful it was to be carried away with the thoughts. I felt that thoughts and emotions controlled me and were so overwhelming. Thoughts always meant something to 'me'. A thought was either a good thought or a bad thought. A thought story was often attached to a certain belief or assumption about 'me'. Thoughts were so important. When I heard that thinking was wrong, this gave the thoughts even more power because each thought had the attached thought, that it is wrong.

Thoughts are simply thoughts. They do not carry any meaning for anyone. They are waves of energy in thought form. Sometimes the wave is very active and sometimes it is in rest.

Thoughts are part of the play that arises and falls away. Each thought, as it happens, is everything and nothing. In between thoughts is just resting. Silence. Potential. And then out of that potential arises thought. There has simply been the assumption that there is never anything but a 'busy mind'. Actually there are so many gaps between thoughts that I don't even notice. But so what if there are no gaps. What I am is not the thoughts, but that which knows all thought. So the thoughts can arise and fall away as much as they like, they never touch what I am.

What does 'mind' mean anyway? There is no such thing as a mind. There are just individual thoughts arising and falling away. There is not a 'mind-entity' which thinks. Since the word 'mind' is used so frequently in speech, there can be the assumption that I am the mind and I think. But where is this mind? Where is this entity? In the brain? I might believe that mind is in the brain, because of what I have learnt from science. Am I in the brain? This is an interesting thought, especially when combined with imagination. But right now, that is all it is—a thought. All I know is this thought. When we say 'the mind' we are actually referring to the thinking process. But even this is not accurate because there is no process. There is only this. This thought. There is only the memory of a previous thought. Actually, all there is, is this thought and now no thought.

Every thought comes from nothing. And in its brief journey in nothing it seeks to return to nothing. Thoughts seem to search for more. More than what is. That is the nature of thought. There is never enough, it is never perfect. The nature of thought is to be agitated, to be in movement. There is nothing wrong with that. There is not less freedom because there is thinking! Thoughts are just phenomena like any appearance. Like a chair or table. They just appear in the play of Life. They arise out of nothing and fall back into nothing. In fact they are nothing appearing as everything in a play with itself.

Labelling

When I see a cat, most of the time there is no thought 'cat'. There is just the seeing of cat. When I feel cold there is not always the thought 'I'm so cold', there is just feeling cold. There is not always the thought 'me'. There is not always the labelling that thought is so good at. In fact the labelling seems to be more of an effort that is added to the simple seeing or feeling. The labelling or defining is that extra effort that seems to be needed in order to survive or interact with the apparent outside world. The simple seeing of this, even the seeing of thoughts which label whatever it is, is it. It's so easy! It's being done already!

The label 'me' could also be called a filter between what is seen to be so private and intimate and the apparently scary outside world. The negotiator with what seems to be the other. The apparent negotiator seems to make everything safe and known. It says 'Don't worry, this is cat.' Or ' Don't worry, this is known and can be labelled'. This seems to make everything safe and known, but all the time, underneath and beyond that, it is already known that there is no safety. There is no negotiator. **There is no 'me' and never has been.**

In recognition of what I am, labelling can go on but there is no relying on it to be a protection from the outside world. It is simply seen for what it is and has always been—just another thought happening in this. There is no inside or outside. There is no 'me' or 'the other'. Even though negotiating can go on, it is always known that there are no boundaries between them. It is all simply playful.

Thought Classifies

Thought is fantastic at classifying and sorting information, images, sensations, emotions, imagination, thoughts, energy. Thought seems to decide that one thought or sensation is better or worse than another. Some thoughts seem to try to push away discomfort and hold on to pleasure. This is what is called in the Eastern traditions 'Samsara' —the wheel of never-ending suffering. It is the endless trying to satisfy the body/mind. This body/mind can never be satisfied. **It is a hopeless case.**

There are thoughts which classify and expand reasons and explanations for emotions that seem to be negative or positive. Thoughts define sadness, anger, happiness, boredom, restlessness, irritation, sexuality, pleasure as different things, which are either good or bad. Also, images of various experiences happening are defined as good or bad: eating a lot, doing some exercise, sitting on the sofa watching TV, going to the pub, giving money to charity, meditating, saying something vulgar, sleeping around.... Physical sensations such as pain or aching or sexual arousal or general restlessness are classified as either something 'I want' or 'I don't want'.

This is the function of thought. It classifies.

Beyond classifying, there is just energy moving and changing. **Body/mind is naturally restless**

and sometimes in discomfort and sometimes pleasure. Any discomfort is bound to change soon and so is any pleasure. Everything is coming and going, arising and falling away. Nothing is constant within the play of what happens. Beyond classifying, I could say that any physical sensation, thought, emotion, imagination, visual image, experience is all one energy that moves around and is interpreted and classified by thought as different things. I could call it all thought: sensation-thought, emotion-thought, imagination-thought, image-thought, experience-thought. They are all just thoughts that come and go. Nothing has any substance. Nothing has any meaning. Nothing is better or worse than anything else. Just as in meditation, when I used to watch my thoughts, as a meditator I knew that no thought had any more value than any other thought. This is the point of meditation—to see that nothing means anything. Actually there is no need to meditate to recognise this.

All this is coming and going, arising and falling away in what? It is all seen to be coming and going by that which does not move. That, which knows all that is impermanent is absolute permanence. This is Life itself. This is silence beyond any experience of silence. Experience of silence just comes and goes. Experience of peacefulness just comes and goes. It can never be relied upon to be constant. The experience of love depends on circumstances for its survival. That which knows experience is empty and does not depend on anything at all. It is overflowing, unconditional love without ever needing to experience love. **Whatever is experienced is always conditional.** The love, peace, silence of experience is only a reflection of that which is absolute. This reflection is absolutely perfect and points directly to that which I am beyond any experience.

The Body/Mind Organism

The body/mind organism is not even that. It is just an image that appears in conjunction with physical sensation and thought. It is all part of the dream. If I close my eyes, there is only the physical sensation of feet on the ground. **There is no body**. Body is just a concept that is assumed. Visual perception can be convincing. If I open my eyes there appears to be an image of body. Then in conjunction with that are the other physical sensations and thought sensations. Actually, it all just appears as part of the play. Image of body, physical sensation and thought are all appearing in absolutely nothing. Where is the physical sensation of feet on the ground happening? It is just assumed to be happening in the body because we assume that there is a body. If I look afresh now, without referring to any memory or assumption, physical sensation is just happening. It is not happening in anywhere. It is just happening in absolute nothingness. The idea of a body is just happening in absolute nothingness. The whole play is just happening in, and as, absolute nothingness.

There is often a physical lack or dissatisfaction felt. I try to fill the lack by searching for that which can fill this endless hole. It can be food, it can be drugs, it can be a lover, it can be a new car, it can be a new career, it can be a spiritual realisation... Some things seem to satisfy this lack for a while and then again it arises in, perhaps, a seemingly different form of dissatisfaction.

The nature of the body/ mind organism is to be dissatisfied. The nature of the body/mind organism is to sometimes feel a lack, to be restless, to be needy, to feel, to sense. This is aliveness. It can be pleasurable or it can be uncomfortable, but is always changing. **Body/mind will never come to a point where it is permanently satisfied**. This is the nature of it. There is nothing to be done about it. It is alive. Only the death of the body can end this and until then there is nothing that can be found to fulfil it, physically, emotionally, mentally or spiritually. There are lots of things that can seem to make the body/mind more comfortable for a while, and of course the tendency is to go for these things but it is questionable that these things can permanently satisfy the body/mind organism.

Everything I try to do is an attempt to satisfy the body/mind organism. Searching for spiritual fulfilment is also that. It is a seemingly more sophisticated way of doing it but actually it is the same thing. With the recognition that there is no way of satisfying the body/mind, there is the realisation that there is no hope and no more belief that there is someone separate who lives in the body who can do anything to change what is happening.

All my life I have been taught and assumed that I am *in* the body and the body has five senses to sense the outside world. Actually this is one of the many assumptions that go unexamined. **There is no one** *in* **the body**. There is no one in the world. I am what knows the appearance of body and the world. The body and the whole world happen in what I am. It is simply assumed that 'I' am in my body. What I am is boundless, limitless. It is the silence that knows all that happens. It is the emptiness in which everything happens. It is the void in which the appearance of the body/mind organism happens. It is that which knows any sensation. If cold is felt, it is not felt in the body, it is just felt. This feeling is simply known in not knowing. There has simply been the blind assumption that it happens 'in my body'. If sadness is felt, it is just felt. If dissatisfaction is felt, it happens nowhere. It is not located anywhere. Visual appearance is the most deceptive because vision is apparently the most reliable sense. We see the appearance of body and we call it 'my body'. The appearance of body is just happening in boundlessness. It is not owned. It is simply seen. This is a completely radically new perspective from the previous assumption. It is no longer an assumption; it is actually the way it is.

Emotion

'I feel a certain peace but it comes and goes. When I get emotional I lose that sense of peace and centredness.' There are so many misconceptions about Enlightenment or Liberation or Life (whatever you want to call it—it doesn't care!).

Emotion seems to rock the boat so much that all there is, is a whirlwind of physical sensations and stories and no awareness of peace and calm. There is also an added story, which implies that there is something wrong with this. Then follows even more emotion and discomfort in the body.

What is the nature of emotion? Emotion is a whirlwind. That is its nature. Emotion can take over logical thought, it can seem overwhelming. Emotion can take over any principles or belief that it is wrong to be un-centred. When there is emotion, there is nothing else.

What does being centred mean? Feeling calm, in control, going with the flow, knowing myself... All of these are either physical sensations, imagination or thought stories happening in that which does not need to know, imagine or feel anything.

When emotion happens, all there is, is emotion. When un-centredness happens, all there is, is un-centredness. There is nothing to be done about this. These are just phenomenon happening as Life.

In fact the nature of Life is un-centred. There is nothing wrong with losing centredness because there is no centre. **Life has no boundaries and no centre.**

The Heart

What is the heart? In school biology lessons we learnt that it is an organ in the body that pumps the blood around the body and that if it should stop, I would die.

In speech we use the word heart when refer-ring to love and kindness. If a person is a heartless person, they are generally considered to be unkind.

In various spiritual teachings, the heart is con-sidered to be an energy centre which is supposed to represent love, truth, a softer feminine side, but most of all the person's centre. If 'I come into my heart' or 'open my heart' then apparently I will be more vulnerable and open to my 'true' feelings.

Actually, what is the heart? It is a word, a con-cept, a memory of a biology lesson, an imagined picture of a body organ associated with the heart-beat that is felt. **I have no heart.**

If the heart is to represent love, I can never have a closed heart. In fact I can never have an open heart, either. Any experience of vulnerability or openness is simply an experience happening in that which can never close. Experience of vulnerability is simply a reflection of the absolute vulnerability of what I am beyond any experience, and has no more or less value than a slice of toast. **What I am is absolute openness, so I never need to try to be open.**

Nothing I do or don't do will have any affect on the opening or connecting with my heart. I am never disconnected from my heart. I am never not in my heart. But this heart is not a centre within my body. In fact the body is an appearance within Heart. Heart is not mine. Heart is boundless. Heart is no one. Heart is the love and vulnerability that is already. Heart is just another word for Life.

Fear

Fear is simply a physical sensation happening. It is often accompanied by thought and emotion, which also simply happen.

Within the play it seems that fear is a holding on to an apparition. It is an apparent contraction from Life. It is a holding on to the known, the recognisable, the definable. The unknown is terrifying to that which proclaims that it knows. It is like a child holding on to its Mummy or Daddy. Mummy and Daddy are what is known, but standing alone without any authority is unknown. Never known.

There is often a pretending to know which covers the fear of not knowing. This pretending holds on for dear life. The apparent person goes to therapy to help create a better-known story to cover the truth that there is no story. Relationships are used as hiding places, and places to create imaginary drama, until there too it is uncovered. It can't hide forever. Eventually the pretence falls apart and it is recognised that nothing can ever be known.

Actually, what I am has no clue. I don't know anything. **I am absolutely lost.** There is only absolutely nothing and in that is the sensation of fear happening.

Confusion and Clarity

Sometimes there seems to be confusion and sometimes clarity. Both confusion and clarity happen as part of the play, which is happening in absolute nothing. When there is confusion there is the belief that this is not *it*. Confusion is taken seriously and can be felt to be wrong. When there is clarity, there is simply clarity happening. Afterwards confusion can arise about the clarity that apparently happened. But still both are simply states happening in this. Absolute nothing, **Life itself, does not care whether there is confusion or clarity**. There is no benefit or value in more clarity than confusion. Both are absolutely what is. Confusion is Life happening as confusion. Clarity is Life happening as clarity. One is not better or worse than the other. Both are states that happen as part of the wave of states that come and go in that which never moves.

It is only the seeker who believes that one is better than the other and therefore something needs to be done about clearing the confusion. Actually, confusion is absolutely perfect, no matter how painful it can feel. Confusion is Life experiencing confusion.

No Way Out

This is it. There is no escape. This is Life. Every step, every thought, every physical sensation, every emotion, every imagination, every spiritual experience, every going to the toilet. This is Life happening. **There is no escape**. There is no escape into alcohol or drugs. There is no escape into sleep. There is no escape by avoiding people or scary situations. Even the avoiding is Life playing at avoiding.

There are no parts or pieces of Life. Life cannot be divided up into sections with boundaries. It only seems to be that way in the play of appearance. The apparent boundaries in the play only seem to separate appearances. Actually it is only Life appearing as an apparent boundary. All appearances are one appearance. One play. There are not parts of Life that are special, and parts which are rubbish. One thing is no better or worse than anything else. Everything that happens is Life living.

A Someone

I have a memory of a conversation with my Dad when I was roughly seven or eight years old. I had come home from school feeling very upset and distressed. I told my Dad that everyone at school seemed to have such strong opinions about everything and I didn't have any opinions about anything. People around me all seemed to have a lot to say about a lot of subjects. I was obviously upset because I thought that I should be like them but didn't know how. My Dad tried his best to help me by asking if I had any opinion about a number of subjects. After a while, he realised that I really had no particular opinion, he suggested that I just make up something original to say.

In this way, I could pretend like everyone else. In an amazingly simple way, probably without realising it, my Dad was showing me that this is all a pretence and that it really does not matter what I say or who I pretend to be. People around me were all pretending to be 'someones'. In order to survive amongst them, I had to pretend as well. Of course, after some time, I began to believe my own pretence. I believed that I was a someone who had a history and a potential future. I believed that things happened 'to me'. I believed that I need to negotiate with the outside world. Separation.

Throughout this apparent time of pretending to be a someone, it was always known beyond it, that this is a pretence. What I am was always privately and intimately known but simply overlooked. The sweet simplicity of not knowing has always been what I am. There was so often the believing that other people must know and I can't possibly know. This was how the knowing of not-knowing was overlooked.

There has never been a someone. Through all the apparent time when I believed I was a some-one, it was simply a belief. So many other beliefs have hung off this belief. So many psychological stories have grown off this belief. When the root dies, the whole tree falls away.

Not-Knowing

I used to think that I should know. I used to think that if I don't know that there was something wrong with me. It seemed as if other people know, but I don't know.

In recognition of what I am, it is seen that I never need to know. Not knowing is what I am. Knowing anything is simply an appearance of knowing, happening in absolute not-knowing.

Not knowing is this. Never knowing. Thoughts try to know. This may never stop because this is the nature of thought. This is all known beyond knowing. Thought continues to try to define and say, "This is it!" It recognises the silence beyond thought and says, "I've got it!" Then this slips away and thought says "Oh no, I've lost it!" It remembers how peaceful and lovely it was and tries to recreate it through imagination. "I must try to hold on to it."

This may all go on, but beyond all this trying to hold on to something imaginary, is the knowing that it can never be held on to. It can never be known, it can never be found, and therefore it can never be lost. It can never be remembered so there is no need to worry about forgetting it. I am lost and forgotten. **Forever lost and never remembered.** This is, eternally, it. Forever falling in not-knowing and never landing.

The Play

Life playing itself. Everything that appears, appears as a caricature of itself. Going to the shop to buy some milk, is so sweet and playful. Pretending to pay for something to a man behind the counter who pretends to put the money in his till. We are like children playing 'going shopping'. Having a serious discussion with someone is hilarious. We pretend to think and talk very seriously about something very important, all the while knowing that it is just a play of sound and we could very well just be saying 'blah, blah, blah' or singing a song. Politics—sweet how they play so seriously. Thoughts tend to be very serious and dramatic. Emotions are so tragic. Life likes to dramatise everything so that it can experience itself as that too. **Thoughts and emotions together create a blockbuster movie!** It's fantastic. Seeking for fulfilment is a very serious game. It involves the blockbuster combination plus some extra spice as well. The seeker goes to a master to be told that she needs to try harder to become better (in whatever technique is recommended), all the while, just behind the pretend seeker, it is known that there is no where to go and nothing to do, but why not play at it anyway! Playing goes on whether it is recognised that it is a play or not. Recognising the play is the play, seeing itself playing.

This play can end at any time. But there is no

player that ends. The movie ends (perhaps in a very tragic ending) but what I am, which has known the movie, has no beginning and no end. There was never a play. There is no play. There is only absolute nothingness, which dreams the play of everything.

Different Roles

Have you ever watched children play? They take on different roles in their play. When they play a role, they are absolutely that role. The child plays Mummy with a doll as baby. She seems so sweet in the totality of what is played. The child plays catching the baddies and totally is the heroic character. Then, they are called in for supper and the parents and child play other roles. The play does not end. We go on playing different roles. In some situations I am extrovert and in others I am very shy. Sometimes I play the emotional character and other times I play the cool detached one. Sometimes I am the teacher and sometimes the student. In a work environment I play another role and at home another. Sometimes there is seriousness and other times light-heartedness. There can be a belief (especially in spiritual circles) that there is something wrong with this changing of roles. I seem to not be true to myself when I adapt to other situations or people. But this is the play of Life. It is ever changing and playing. **There is no constant, consistent character**. There is no consistent self to be true to. There is only Life, which knows each role. It is Life playing through each unique perception.

Choice

There is never any choice. Choice is a concept based on the idea that there is a separate someone who can choose. If I have a look at the most simple action that appears to have choice involved, it is obvious that there is no question of a choice. I decide that it is a good idea to bend my finger. If I think that it is right and best and even morally correct to bend my finger, this all has no connection to the actual finger-bending. Finger-bending happens out of nothing, as nothing finger-bending.

Whatever I think I decide to do is a thought that simply arises and then falls away. Doing happens or not.

Thoughts seem to be so connected to the finger-bending that it seems that they actually make it happen. Thoughts are running alongside what happens as a commentary: "That was a really well-bent finger, I am really good to have bent my finger, now other people will think I'm good", "Mine was the worse bent finger in the class. I will probably never be able to bend my finger like her." This commentary can be given so much importance and is so strongly believed in. It is actually believed that this thought or action means something to 'me'.

The thought "I am doing this" is just a thought that actually has no connection to the action that happens. The "I am doing this" thought is based on the "I am a someone" thought or belief. In the belief in a separate someone, it appears that that someone can choose to do or not to do. What I am is not a belief or assumption or thought. **What I am is the nowhere in which things simply happen in absolute meaninglessness.**

The Paradox

In recognition of Life itself, there is no choice, nothing happening, no individual, no separation, no knowing, and yet it seems as if there is a separate individual who chooses things that happen. This is the paradox that does not seem to make sense. There is nothing I can do to change anything and yet changes happen. There is no one who does anything and yet it appears that 'I' do things. It feels as if 'I' am in control of what happens but actually everything simply happens.

It seems as if recognition of what I am is a something that happens to a someone in the play. But this recognition has nothing to do with what happens. This is the most amazing paradox because it so often seems as if 'I' can do something to improve what is. 'I' can try to be more authentic, or more meditative but this is all part of the play. The play of Life itself, playing the individual. The play that is running with no controller. Everything simply happening for no one.

This is only recognised in not understanding. How different it is from everything else that we know that happens in the play. If we try to understand a philosophy we can have a clearer and more logical perspective of it. But this is not a philosophy; this has nothing to do with someone understanding something. This has nothing to do with any kind of change or improvement. This has nothing to do with getting or becoming something. This is the absolute paradox of what is already.

Acceptance and Unconditional Love

The seeker often hears that 'Awakening' or 'Enlightenment' is absolute acceptance and unconditional love and so tries to *do* these. The seeker tries to accept everyone and not judge them. The seeker tries to love and never hate. The seeker tries to accept whatever happens and not get annoyed. There is the belief that acceptance and unconditional love are right and judgement, hate, and annoyance are all wrong.

There is no right or wrong. There is only what is. Acceptance and unconditional love can't be done. If there is hate, there is hate. If there is annoyance or judgement, then this is what is. What I am is freedom that is non-exclusive. Judgement, frustration, irritation, hate, anger are Life happening as that. This is freedom that includes whatever happens. Thoughts qualify what is good or bad. The function of thought is to qualify. What is being pointed to is a leap beyond thought. In the recognition of this, unconditional love is recognised. Unconditional love is, despite feeling hatred or judgement. Unconditional love does not care about what happens in the play. It has no interest in whether the character feels kindness or hatred. It doesn't care about apparent atrocities committed. It doesn't care that you don't give money to charity. It doesn't care whether people die or starve; it has no interest in whether you do apparent 'good' or kind deeds. Kindness can happen. Love can happen but this does not mean anything. This is Life happening. Nothing means anything. It is all a play of absolutely everything which is known, in impersonal unconditional love.

What I am is absolute humility. What I am is absolute innocence. What I am is absolute accept- ance and unconditional love. **I don't have to try to be all this because what I am is all this already**.

Relationship

There is never any relationship. "You" and "me" are both just ideas that arise in emptiness. When two apparent people meet we are only pretending to meet—actually, in reality, we were never apart and so can never meet.

When I love someone, sometimes I long to be close to them, so close that I actually want to climb into them! Physical intimacy just never seems to be close enough. In fact in relationship there is always a 'lack' of some kind. It is never good enough or close enough.

Generally, women tend to fear losing themselves in relationship, and men fear being engulfed by or 'falling into' the other. Both are games of protection that are played to avoid being absolutely lost. The losing of the illusion of a separate self. At the same time as the fear of losing oneself, there is a longing for it as well. This is the paradox of seeking for fulfilment in the ideal relationship. This is the terrible pain of it. Both games are the attempt to hold back and hide away from becoming the other. Believing that it is possible to protect, and knowing that the games of protection might be exposed seems terrifying. Both players pretend to be separate, knowing beyond that, that there is actually no separation. They play their games, but in love the boundaries melt and it is seen that there are no boundaries, there is no separation. **The apparent two lovers fall into none**. There is only absolute love happening.

There is no one to relate or to relate to. Whoever (or whatever) I meet, I have never been separate from. There is no need to try to become closer because there is only ever Love. Getting closer happens in the play, without the feeling of needing to fulfil a sense of loss. No more hiding and protecting. There is no one to hide from and no one to hide. There is never any relationship. It is all over. Only a celebration of love is left.

The Male/Female Thing

We might have heard the explanation of the meeting of the male and female energy that merges into one in 'Enlightenment'. Apparently in Tantric teachings, if the male and female join in true lovemaking, they can go beyond their separate bodies and become one in a holy union. This seems all very spiritual but actually **this is the way it is already**. There is no male or female. These are only appearances in a play of duality and opposites. **Male and female have never not been one**. In the play there is the game of opposites coming together and moving away. But actually, there is already only absolute union. There is nothing to be done. No right lovemaking can bring you closer to union when this is it already. Lovemaking is a beautiful play and is just as significant as boiling the kettle. This union has nothing to do with being in any kind of relationship or being either male or female or even being particularly holy! It has nothing to do with the play at all.

What I am is absolutely complete and unified. There is no need to try to become one. **I am both male and female and neither male nor female.**

Love

Love has no boundaries. Love has no limits. Love has no definition or qualities. Love is not a 'thing'. It is not tangible. It cannot be described except by saying what it is not. Love has no timeframe. Love is beyond a concept of time. Love is the substance of Life and Death. All that appears is **Love happening**. In no appearance there is only Love. Love cannot be grasped by thought. But thought tries relentlessly to grasp it, to understand it and confine it. But Love doesn't care about thoughts. Love is, despite a thought that it is not. There is no fear in Love. There is simply a resting, a relaxation beyond any possible relaxation of the body. Love is the fire and passion which bubbles over all boundaries. It knows no principles or morals. It does not have reasons. Love is Life happening. There is nowhere to go but Love. No escape from Love.

Vertical Not Horizontal

This is it. This is like a spear vertically cutting through a horizontal timeline. There is no horizontal timeline. There is no past or future. There is no before or after. Any moment just before this one is just a memory or thought. Any thought about the past happens vertically in this. Whatever happened just before this, never happened. In the same way, nothing will ever happen. There is no future. Any future is just imagination happening vertically in this.

There is only ever the vertical spear, which ridicules a horizontal timeline. A belief in a horizontal timeline seems to imply a continuation of this. A string of 'this's' linked together. This belief makes it seem as if there is a connection between one 'this' and another, but in 'this' there is never another! Any other moment is just a thought happening in this.

A horizontal timeline can be understood. It can feel safe and secure. One event logically leads to the next. Cause and effect. If I push a door, it will close. But actually there is only pushing. In 'pushing' there is never anything else. In the imagination of 'door closing' there is only imagination and it does not lead to the door actually closing. This cannot be understood and is certainly not logical. It is absolute insecurity. Nothing is going anywhere. *This* **is not leading to** *that.* This is it! The whole of Life and Death is in whatever this is. This is the beginning and the end.

Death

There is no Death. Who is going to die? Who has ever lived? No one has ever lived or has ever been born. Life just happens. There is no time line with a beginning, middle and end. There is only this. There is only an appearance of a body. There is only a story that this appearance was born. Death is only a thought story. Thoughts take the idea of Death and make it into such an exciting story. Really Death is just the end of the assumption that there is a some-one who owns Life. It's the end of the story of 'me' and 'my life'.

When this assumption is believed, it creates a whole perspective. Everything is seen through this assumption of a 'me'. There is a contracted view of all that appears. 'My' life, 'my' body, 'my' lover, 'my' child, 'my' day, 'my' friend...etc. Or not mine. There is a fear which separates one into many. This idea of 'me' is terrified of Death because it will be the end of it. This contracted perspective seems safe. There is always a knowing of the vast expansiveness of what is beyond all assumptions and because it is known, it is also feared. A lot of effort is seemingly put into avoiding Death at all costs.

This Death does not only happen when the apparent body dies. With recognition of the nature of Life, there is the Death of the belief in the story of 'me'. This is how in recognition of what I am, I can say that I have already died. **Life may go on but there is no one living**. In fact there was no one living even before this recognition. It was just assumed that there was a 'someone' who lives and who will die. This assumption is seen for what it is—an assumption only. What I am never dies. What I am has never been born.

Freedom

Not knowing. That is the nature of this. Thoughts and words always try to know and control. What knows all this is simple innocent not-knowing. There is absolute freedom in not-knowing. Freedom of never needing to know. Freedom beyond the concept of freedom. This is a freedom beyond any appearance of suffering or bondage. Freedom beyond the sweet pleasures that come and go and can never be held on to. Freedom beyond any belief in a someone to be free. This is freedom beyond understanding, beyond explanations. **I don't know why or how I am free, but I am freedom itself!!!!**

Maturity

I always used to think of being mature as taking responsibility for my actions. Being serious. I often put others up on pedestals and assumed that they must know, and I don't know. I assumed that others must be right without even checking what I already know. This view was based in fear. There is only innocent not knowing. Nothing in this play is known, even though people go around pretending that they know so much.

Maturity is recognising that there is no authority. There is no one who knows. The truth is that no one knows anything. Only in not knowing, this is all known. Innocent not knowing is what I am. The rest is just a pretence. Maturity is the realisation that there is no mother or father. I am absolutely alone. I can no longer simply believe what others say or do. I can no longer believe a philosophy or spiritual teaching. I can no longer believe in the pretence. I am ready to see what is really the case. I am the only authority and only in not knowing, I know.

Maturity is the readiness to wake up from the dream. Maturity is the recognition that I have never been anything but child-likeness.

Child-likeness

Recognition of Life itself reveals the innocence or child-likeness that has always been, but has been simply overlooked. This innocence is recognised as what I am beyond a contracted perspective of 'me'. The innocence that I am has always been, even when it seemed to be overlooked.

Whatever happens, happens in meaninglessness, as it does for a child. Everything is unique and new. There is a living in surprise at whatever happens. Life is playing at being a character. The character is played through. There is no illusion of any control. There is only seeing what happens. The character plays different roles and adapts to different situations. There is never any fixed character, which can be identified. There is a responding to situations with no holding on to anything. Like a child who cries but then immediately smiles when it notices something moving in front of it. The tears are immediately forgotten and what is now is the object moving in front of its face.

A flow of sensations arising. A flow of energy appearing. A flow of energy appearing as something. A flow of energy happening in nothing.

This Is It

This is not going anywhere. This is the beginning and the end. This is it. There is nothing more or less. This is the whole of Life and Death. There is no journey. This is it. There is nowhere else. This has always been it. There never has been a past and will never be a future. **This is all that has ever been longed for.** This is it. This is all that has ever been hoped for. There is no hope. Hope implies movement to a future. There is no movement. This is it. There is no need. There is no lack. This is absolutely empty but at the same time absolutely full. This is it. There is no point. There is no trying to become. This is wholeness and nothing. This is the end of the search. This is it.

Contraction and Expansion

Nothing is happening. Paradoxically, it seems as if there are many things happening. One thing that seems to have happened over an apparent period of time is an expansion. In the story of time, there used to be no trust in that which I have always known I am. I went through life believing that I was wrong and others must be right. I was looking 'out there' for the answers. That which I have always known but not trusted, was believed to be a separate 'me' who felt contracted and was assumed to be 'in' the body. In recognition of Life itself, there is not simply trust in that, but only that, which I have always known. There seemed to be an expansion, as beliefs and assumptions were seen through. The boundaries of inside and outside melted into none.

There were never any boundaries. In fact there was no expansion because there was never really any contraction. How can I contract and expand when I am all that is, which has no boundaries? This is the paradox. A story of things happening, to describe nothing happening. A story in time, to describe that which is timeless.

Ordinariness

Life is so simple. So ordinary. The recognition of Life's ordinariness is what some people call Enlightenment or Liberation. These are really fancy names for what is so ordinary and has always been known. What I am has simply been overlooked in the expecting to find something more special. Everything that happens, a rose bud opening—thoughts create a dramatic story around it. 'Oh isn't that beautiful, isn't it romantic' or even a scientific explanation. Thoughts never seem to be satisfied with the simple seeing of this. This ordinariness. It is never quite good enough. With the extra story, thoughts make it seem special. In fact beyond this extra story, **everything is beautifully naked** and there is only clear and simple Life happening.

Everything is what it is, just the way it is. A rose bud is just a rose bud. It does not need any addition of a thought to make it more special. It is absolutely unique in its simple ordinariness.

Life is described as ordinary only in comparison to how special thoughts make it seem sometimes. Actually, nothing is ordinary about it. It is all so buzzing with Life that it sometimes seems that it is about to explode with simple aliveness!

Too Simple

Nothing to say and no one to say it. Saying can happen but no one says anything. Not saying can happen but there is no one to decide whether to say or not say. Everything happens in its ordinary simplicity. Nothing is special but at the same time everything is special. Beyond imagination and ideas of what it is. It's much too simple for that. Only boundlessness. Only limitlessness. Only freedom. Only Life happening. Nothing to lose. Never born and already died.

Joy beyond ever needing to be joyful. Love beyond ever needing to be loving. Silence beyond ever needing quiet. Stillness beyond the stillness of body or mind. Gentle but can be ruthless. Compassion beyond ever needing to be nice. Peace throughout any war. Truly free despite any walls. Freedom beyond physical freedom. The only authority beyond any authority. No limits. Beyond any experience whether spiritual, physical, emotional or mental. The end of hope. Death. So beyond words that every word seems to be a lie. But still, words happen. It cannot help but overflow into expression. Innocence. Sweetness. Intimacy. Strength. All qualities and no quality. Not ever needing to be a particular quality. No-thing. Nothing beyond any imagination of nothing. This is what I am. **Absolutely lost to all that is found**. Never knowing. Roaring in not-knowing.

The rebellious, radical roar of Life!

Raw Open Wound

I am a raw open wound. There are no filters that filter off what I don't want or want to feel. Pain, sadness, joy, sexuality, mischievousness, curiosity... It is all felt like a wound. It arises and then falls away in nothing. There is no ownership of any sensation. There is no protection of the wound. So much energy is freed up that was once used in protecting the belief in a someone, that whatever is felt is simply felt by no one. Everything is alive and vibrant but with no drama. Feeling is simply feeling. **So what?** Joy is simply joy. Pain is simply pain. It arises and falls away and there is no one to own it or to move towards it or away from it. It is all simply sensation happening in what I am.

Possibilities

Tinkling of water. Breathing in the smell of roses. Stroking a purring cat. Watching the sunrise over the sea. Melting in the eyes of a lover. Hearing a baby giggle. Tears of heartbreak. Looking in the mirror at a little girl who feels lost. This is Life. Life is limitless possibilities. Possibilities of joy or despair. Possibilities of beauty or ugliness. Possibilities of love or hate. Possibilities of overwhelming emotion or numbness. Possibilities of intellectualising or intuition. Possibilities of male or female. Possibilities of old or young. Possibilities of this one or that one. **It is limitless**. Anything can and does happen.

In this play of time, all the possibilities happen and then stop happening and then another possibility happens and then stops happening and another and another... It is a constant flow of happenings that come and go like a fluid stream. Some are very quick to happen and then stop happening, and others happen for longer. Enjoying a piece of chocolate cake comes and goes quite quickly, but this body happening seems to last longer.

Gratitude

This has always been known since a child. The absolute sweet nature of what I am beyond any pretence. As the character was born and was cultivated, qualities grew and took fruit. In recognition of the nature of Life, that always was, is the absolute gratitude to, and as, this, which never left. This, which was never touched by any qualities or cultivation. This, which seemed to wait patiently to be found. This, which has never been lost and never needed to be found. To this, there is an overflowing gratitude from no-one to no-one. To this, that always was and always will be. To this, which is beyond any concepts of complication and confusion. To this which knows and adores all concepts and complication. To this, which can never be described, no matter how many words. To this, which is all words and no word. To this, that I am, Life itself, there are tears of overflowing gratitude.

For further information about meetings with Unmani, and to contact the author, please visit: www.not-knowing.com

020 8838 1819
unmanicool@yahoo.co.uk